**ANCHOR BOOKS**

WHISPERS IN THE WIND

Edited by

Sarah Andrew

First published in Great Britain in 2001 by
ANCHOR BOOKS
Remus House,
Coltsfoot Drive,
Peterborough, PE2 9JX
Telephone (01733) 898102

HB ISBN 1 85930 990 9
SB ISBN 1 85930 995 X

FOREWORD

Anchor Books is a small press, established in 1992, with the aim of promoting readable poetry to as wide an audience as possible.

We hope to establish an outlet for writers of poetry who may have struggled to see their work in print.

The poems presented here have been selected from many entries. Editing proved to be a difficult task and as the Editor, the final selection was mine.

I trust this selection will delight and please the authors and all those who enjoy reading poetry.

Sarah Andrew
Editor

CONTENTS

CHOICES

I took my first breath, I've joined the human race,
I didn't choose the time, I didn't choose the place,
I didn't choose my mum, I didn't choose my dad,
I didn't choose my doctor, he's the one they've always had.

I didn't have a say about my nursery or school,
My mum put me right, she would, my mum's no fool,
She knew what was best for me, she gave me all she could,
My parents chose all these things, but then I knew they would.

Now I've grown up, I've made choices of my own,
Many have been wrong, but I know I'm not alone,
With choices came mistakes, lots of them, I'm sure you know,
I hope the same won't happen as I watch my children grow.

I watch them do many things that I have done before,
Just like me they won't be told, they know best and that's for sure,
So I'll let them get on with it, I gave them life to live,
I hope they don't live for taking, I hope they've learnt to give.

When they have children of their own, I'll know they'll understand,
You don't get what you want from life, by holding out your hand,
It doesn't come that easy you have to work at it, you'll see,
That goes for everyone that's born, not just for you or me.

Elaine Chaplin

DARK SONNET

You stand, stare out of the window,
behind you, someone sits and cries,
it's over.

Can pretend no longer,
keep thinking about all those good times we had,
that now I find only bad.

Cut and run,
so much easier said than done,
cannot go on living,
this sad, sad lie.

No wish to hurt you,
please, don't cry.

Have to leave
have to say goodbye . . .

Susan Barker

RESPONSIBILITY

The Media screams of violence and crime,
Of hunger, floods, of poverty and drought.
We sit, and watch the massacre of time
And wonder, vaguely, what it's all about.
And through our mighty, awe-inspiring land
Stalks anger, and we feast on death and lies.
The world revolves, the fires of hate are fanned
While mothers sing their pointless lullabies
To naked babes, their innocence displayed
Toward the shining stars and velvet black
Of night, and greet their future we have made.
We see our feverish Earth, and turn our back.
But wherein lies responsibility?
Perhaps the finger points at you and me.

Lisa Falshaw

It's Only The Lonely

Enigmatic, precise, suffocating;
Constant fear of neglect and rejection.
Reads a book, while waiting at the station.
Edgy, nervous and constantly fiddling.

Lights a cigarette, with perfect timing.
Down comes the train, he walks in slow motion.
Eyes empty seat and assumes position.
Avoids contact and carries on reading.

Reaches destination, eyes straight ahead,
Longs to get home to relax and take rest.
He stumbles and falls and stratches his head;
Rises to his feet his hair in a mess;
Young lady asks about cut on his head,
Hesitating, he thinks; this is the test.

Harold Winterbottom

SPLIT SECOND PHONE CALL

If truth be told it has been a long time,
quite honestly, in fact, we're talking years;
at first it swamped my raw and confused mind
and frequently engendered mournful tears.

The analgesic months managed to burn
from memory, the face we knew so well;
the drip and feed was slow and reconfirmed
that solely now within our thoughts you dwell.

Forgetful present trips us up, it seems,
it flicks and reels to catch us unaware,
we grow accustomed in our fitful dreams
but sitting up full-conscious in a chair?

I thought last night, out of nowhere at all,
it's been ages since I gave Dad a call.

Philip Huckle

THE LOVEABLE OTTER

Inquisitive brown whiskered face
Darting all over the place
Ever twitching little nose
Pointing upwards as he goes
Sliding in the quiet stream
Making rings of water gleam
Searching for his next fish meal
Something tasty like an eel.
Otter playing on the bank
With his mate - up to their pranks
Otter with your charming way
We love to watch you swim and play
Though dwindling now to just a few
Countryside won't be the same without you.

Jennifer Payne

THE CHALLENGE

The future is in God's hands,
But we must play our part,
By giving loyal service,
And an ever loving heart.

Now looking to the future
There's so much to be done,
But with God's help we'll do it,
There is a job for everyone.

God gave us all a talent,
Some of them quite rare,
So use them for his service, and
Remember the power of prayer.

His promise will sustain us,
As along the way we tread,
He knows it is not easy
So 'He' goes on ahead.

Through times of joy and hardship,
His presence is ever near,
He joins with us in laughter,
And wipes away the tear,

Now if you think this poem,
Could not apply to you,
Remember every little helps,
Do not leave it to a few.

Will A Tilyard

REQUIESCAT IN PACEM

In twilight once again, all wellness fled,
I see what should have been my life recede,
And hope and joy and aspiration bleed
Away and leave sick limbs and heart and head.
An ancient Requiem plays by my bed;
Serene and lovely, glorying in their creed
The polyphonic voices intercede
For peace and sleep for souls of the long-dead.
To be with them would sometimes seem my choice -
With those old spirits seek my final rest
To leave this pain and seek the balm they give;
But I still heed the strong, deep-calling voice -
The heart which chants to me within my breast
The miracle: 'You live! You live! You live!'

David Lees

LOST IN A SONG

How beautiful the life that voice gives verse
How easily your will and mind are swayed
The words seduce you from reality, and worse
With each beguiling note that's gently played.
With your eyes you see all that's in your day
But close them, to better hear the tune
And with them closed you see another way.
Lose yourself in its promise and perfume
Let your heartbeat rise and fall with every note
All your senses tricked and teased into belief.
Then awake once more, come back from what he wrote.
The singer is an artist and a thief.

Painting pictures in your dreams of hope or sorrow
And keeping them, to tempt you with tomorrow.

S P Oldham

SPAN

The creeping tide of ochre dawn,
Devours the canopy of night
Blots out the lantern of man's dreams
Splats promises of pure gold light.
A million dusky silver eyes
Have blinked their last, round father's cusp
Though even he succumbs to glimpse
The fiery hand, its fingers thrust.
The jaws of earth are yawning wide,
Vast spirits raised by heat drenched light
This day will yield abundantly -
Till spent - and day gives way to night.

In gardens lush, dials lit by sun
Reduce the golden miles by one!

Brenda Mentha

STREET SHADOWS

There is a street, a lonely street,
Where men in pit clogs used to meet,
Women put down their work to chat,
Over wooden fences at the back,
Privet hedges trimmed so neat,
Roses with horse manure at their feet.
Children gathered on a starry night
Beneath the gas lamp's friendly light,
Sounds of laughter filled this street,
Kick off can, hop-scotch, hide and seek.

Now the hedges are gone to make room for cars,
Only silence walks under the stars,
Men, women, working to meet their aims,
Children playing computer games.

Joan Egan

SWEET ONE

Tranquillity of cat upon my knee,
Who softly rumbles forth deep-throated purr,
I stroke his head, he stretches sleepily,
My fingers roam through soft and silky fur,
He looks at me through half-closed golden eyes,
Enjoying fuss as only cats know how,
And I enjoy the comfort as he lies
Across my lap so warm and cuddly now;
Contentment is a cat beside the fire,
Ensconced in cosy armchair here with me,
To be adored and fed are his desire,
And in return he'll love me constantly,
But cats aren't owned I know for certainty,
He'll soon be off to wander out and free.

Ailsa Keen

IDEAL WORLD

In an ideal world there would be no crime
No muggings, no theft, no fraud or abuse
No embezzlement in a world sublime
No misappropriation or misuse

In an ideal world everyone would pray
There was peace and total tranquillity
Where children would laugh and be happy in play
Knowing there's an air of stability

In an ideal world there would be no drugs
If only we could live in harmony
Where teenagers would be safe, free from thugs
But it's only a dream, a fantasy

So we make the most of what life brings us
Living in a world that is contentious.

Phyllis L Stark

A WALK ON THE WILD SIDE

Foot and mouth has taken a hold
Spreading faster than the common cold
The countryside is not the same
As if someone has been and put out the flame
Cattle in sheds, sheep in pens,
Animals shut up in their dens
Feeding the ducks is strictly taboo
No more throwing bread for a week or two
Ramblers are barred, walking is stuted
Anyone caught will be prosecuted
Farmers are prisoners on their own estate
Cannot go beyond the gate
Spring is here fields of daffodils,
Lambs should be grazing on the hills,
A walk on the wild side is no more
Unless you wipe your feet at the door.

Margaret Land

TRAPPED INSIDE JUST A MOMENT

Enchained in a locked-up printout prison
A cell with only your thoughts together
Within one place to madness be driven
Inside one frame of stillness forever

Captured with a flash, now here in this place
Frozen inside an infinite occasion
Aching strains in the smile on your face
Flat in a world of endless duration

No change, the same weather, with you within
A method to recall moments at ease
Large eyes, over peering, at you they grin
Remembering past times: your family

Sealed in a picture is your resting tomb
Sitting on a shelf in the dining room.

Joe Reese (16)

AS SUNSET STEALS

A tree stately.
So much serene confidence;
Would think naivety's stable,
But if truth, be proud, a dance.

Standing there, free.
Not the breeze, ruffles;
Neither downpours, a spree.
The indomitable, buffles.

As sunset steals,
Finds nobility, in shadowed depth.
Comes into itself, and feels;
All the meaning, a breath.

Tree of stature,
Confident of capture.

Rowland Warambwa

WHATEVER HAPPENED TO MAY?

What happened to the laughing child of May,
With curls and rosy cheeks and sparkling eyes,
And charm and pleasingness to mesmerise?
Her looks of innocence would well portray
A child like any other at her play;
But guileless looks of righteousness disguise
A nature born to hurt and tantalise.
Who took May's sweet simplicity away?

Why did she cause such sadness and despair
To those who loved her unrestrainedly?
Why do young blossoms die when given care,
Compassion change into antipathy?
So many expectations once were there;
What turned such promise into tragedy?

Hilary J Cairns

THE RAPE OF SPRING

With tragic gaze and grief too hard to bear,
a sturdy farmer bows his head to weep
for farms bereft of soft-eyed cattle's stare.
No lambs breathe spring among his bleating sheep.

Cliff paths are closed above the ancient church
that prays in bleak despair above the beach
of wind-swept sand that feet may not besmirch
whilst summer meadows cower out of reach.

An acrid stench of burning fills the air
from blazing flesh that fuels funeral pyres.
Spring fields must waste, though lush and greenly fair,
stark hedges totter, raped by Hell's grim fires.

Poor Earth that suffers floods, disease and vice!
Poor beasts that die in fear to pay the price!

Ruby Midwinter

THE ELEPHANT

(Dedicated to Mr and Mrs Bohane:
Aunt Floss, Uncle Dan: Deceased)

The elephant's right leg is lifted high.
I trod on the shadow of your balloon
But God was with me in the church at noon.
The brown, thin winged, starlings rush the sky
Above the red slate sunlight of July.
I saw those celluloid shrouds, the monsoon
Of Hiroshima, they became maroon.
I did some shopping late, don't ask me why.
I purchased Radio and TV Times,
Ten Donner Express steaks, two loaves of bread,
Bananas, apples and grapes off the vines,
Potatoes, carrots, pencils made of lead,
Vinegar, washing powder, cooking salt,
Walked out the shop saw an assault.

Edmund Saint George Mooney

DEAR MUM

Now the bowl is filling and filling high,
Is it now soon for I grow restless
For triumph beneath a vengeful sky
And my joyous line in a mournful press.

Where have your drunk immoral looks now gone
That shaped my future from my hour of birth,
Into a living death where no light shone
And shame that I walk upon this earth.

I'm your son still you drank and fought so well,
Upstairs in my world of sorrow and fear
My youth faded to the bosom of hell,
Save for a child's promise made so dear.

The day your aged hand reaches out for mine
My promise is fulfilled, and I can watch you die.

Paul Stuart

BOOKWORM

I move around from shelf to shelf and find,
in each crammed row, a book which I desire;
then choose the next companion for my mind
and follow plots in which I can conspire.

For I observe the characters and live
their lives and see each place and hear each sound;
all gained from books (just black on white) that give
such joy to millions since the first was bound.

Yet now the literary form must change,
some say, exemplifying high-tech ways
from which anachronistic pages range
and take up too much space and time these days.

But I don't want to lose the book's rewards,
to curling up with modems or keyboards.

Peter Gould

WHY ME?

You asked me 'Why?' and I replied 'Why not?',
The day is dark and full of stress,
We ask it oft' when we must face our lot,
I ask it of myself I do confess.

It's how you can deal with the tests of life,
That build and strengthen your innermost soul,
It's not only you that is dealt out strife,
It's up to you how you use it to grow.

To get the best from the way that we live,
Depends on how we turn despair to hope,
Relies on questions and answers we give,
And how we work at a way to cope.

Ask, what can I do? How can I address?
Have I endeavoured and given my best?

Kate Laity

CREATIVITY BONUS

Rich plump Eden, perfect holy land torn
By flawed notion. Friday lunchtime joke. Man
Bitter parting shot, a manic God's plan
Who sneaked away head down, bonus well borne
Such guilt he carries who made us with scorn
Allowed mighty egos to conquer, span
The globe crushing beneath. The coward ran
Forsook his project without grace to mourn

Yet we desired knowledge, questioned nature
Longed bite the poison apple, fall from grace
Pushed beyond programme certain to endure
Statues shout greatness, science conquered space
Great books delight, teach. Medics illness cure
Assign blame? Applaud our faults, unique race.

Elaine Lovegrove

AGEING GRACEFULLY

Noble maple tree in your slenderness,
Swaying gracefully, supple in the breeze,
Exquisite pale green leaves of tenderness,
Shimmering shyly amidst ancient trees.

Standing straight and tall in firm erectness,
Proudly tossing your creamy gold tresses,
Limbs all-acquiver in sensuousness,
Foliage swirling like young girls dresses.

Glorious golden tree of youthfulness,
Yielding pliantly beneath the hills,
In fullness of vigour and hopefulness,
Eternally will you hear a bird's trills.

Ageless, I yearn to prolong life like you,
Ever lost in the beauty of your view.

Betty Mealand

THE TEMPEST

Shakespeare's play was of an exciting theme.
To most people a storm will cause alarm.
All of his work was held in high esteem.
Mostly before a storm there comes a calm.

In cyclone and tornado the wind will scream
Some chase the eye of a storm without qualm.
This whirlwind seems to be an American dream.
It's amazing more don't come to harm.

Blood-red sky and seas herald India's monsoon.
Land heat sucks cool from seas in giro system.
Turmoil in a hurricane and a typhoon.
The sea is a whirlpool of a Maelstrom.
Desert dust devils swirl in a vortex simoon.
Wind, rain, hail or snow it's never hum-drum.

Irene S Hinton

HISTORY

Barrow-in-Furness, where's past glory gone?
Iron-ore once its staple industry
shipping and world trade greatness all now done?
Not true - alive in Dock Museum - see?
Yorkshire's vast coal mines are now all but closed
to say nothing of those elsewhere - vacant -
role still in mining museum - work posed.
Agricultural museum - live slant
into the methods that once made profits;
York has its rail museum - going where?
Burnley's Weavers' Triangle great past quits.
Manchester had Museum of Labour.
Is everything depicting lost greatness?
Nothing good real any more, loss and less?

Robert D Shooter

WHAT ENTAIL FROM THOSE HEAVY, SNOW-BOUND SKIES?

What entail from those heavy, snow-bound skies
Thrusts trysting, trusting, slowed-down, sun-gowned trees
To brushing their hair, as the dancing breeze
Prances brashly by, bearing spring's green prize?

Spring brings brighter days, and new hopes arise.
Low-bent, sloped, proud and patient old pear trees
Bear early blooms for eager, questing bees;
The resting moon smiles, and the March night flies!
Arch primroses wait early by the gate;
Late melting snows pale, probing shoots conceal -
But soon reveal life that the sun's strength lifts.

Gifted spring and summer anticipate
Fruits of harvest - produce of autumn's fields -
Yields in entail . . . old winter's bequeathed gifts.

Dan Pugh

COMING TO BLOWS

Winds like man's nature blow both hot and cold,
Ingratitude may greet the flowers of spring,
March winds can change from light to fierce and bold,
Like elephants when they charge trumpeting.

Blowing a fortune on a game of chance,
Life's lottery all farmers sadly know,
Yet creating a natural balance,
Needs patience, skill and grace of God to grow.

The wind blows little boats across the sea,
Above the wrecks where gold finders have dived,
Whales from the ocean depths blow fearlessly,
Fountains that dance, air that is enlivened.

Seedlings and leaves are blown and summer roses,
Hoping for better times, dry eyes, blow noses.

Kathleen Mary Scatchard

TORTOISE-TRUTH

The pace of modern life will be its doom,
Its curse, the pressure to maintain the pace,
'Victim of speed' is written on our tomb,
The tortoise not the hare will win the race.
Fast-lane fatigue, computer-fault delay
And rush-hour standstill ape the erratic hare
Who sped and slept and lost; we lose today,
All haste, no gain, no time to stand and stare.
What is this life? No time to take repose
With rapid rate of change, fast-track careers;
This cult of speed insidiously sows
The seeds of illness borne in later years.
Heed tortoise-truth and let our children see
Life's race is won in slow serenity.

Janet Forrest

NIL BY MOUTH

The minute hand drags backwards through her hair
entwined in roots the follicles distend.
Her eyes are focused, deep, yet distant stare
as time reverses slowly to the end.

No ringing tone - no text - no answerphone:
regurgitating silence chews her brain.
The bass pipe of her heart expels a drone
transcribed on graph - excruciating pain.

And to the end he lied right from the start.
Orgasmic member spilled the seeds of love,
their cries of satisfaction pierced her heart:
she shared their *ecstasy* but not enough.

Her lips betrayed, she utters not a word
but in his conscience every thought is heard.

Susan Seward

HANDS OF LOVE

Grasp my hand tight my love; don't let it go,
For when you do I'll know that you have gone,
Grasp my hand tight, for I do love you so,
Then I can fool myself that they were wrong.

Reflecting on you when you were so well,
Smiling, laughing, your eyes sparkling so blue,
Full of the zest for life, no one could tell,
This darkness was growing inside of you.

Love hold my hand, you're starting to lose grip,
And I can't bear the thought - letting you pass,
Darling, suffer no more - I feel you slip,
Free, free from pain that's haunted you, at last.

Promise we made - I will fully fulfil,
Heaven we'll meet - hold hands once more we will.

Sarah Hibbett

SNOWDON SONNET

With ghosts of miners from forgotten days
We both stride out with sacks upon our backs
Along the gently sloping miners' tracks.
The eastern sky is clear of smudging haze
And Lliwedd's chiselled cloudless cliffs do soar,
But westward Crib Goch's spine is hung with shrouds,
Its pinnacles and peaks now lost in clouds
And promise of clear summit views, no more.
The marker stone beside the railway's steel
Urges a quickening to stodgy pace.
The misty summit's near in time and space
With lofty loco's steam and brakes that squeal.
We rest by stone-girt trig midst crusted snow,
And see, through japanned clouds, our way below.

Alan Day

MIRROR IMAGE

I see reflections in my mirror small,
What life would be if people had respect.
An ideal world, there is no pain at all,
No sorrow, heartache, misery, neglect.

I dance in dreams, where fantasies are live,
I have no say so have no faults or blame,
But now we have control, we can survive,
Yet only if we try to douse the flame.

I hope that in the years that lie ahead
That my reflections change to what is here.
No pain, no hurt, no tears or lies or dread,
But freedom, hope and all that we hold dear.

I want to see a happy, hopeful earth,
Of joy, of love, of peacefulness and mirth.

Athalia Pyzer

THE FORESTWIFE

Step softly if you tread the secret way
beneath the ancient trees which guard this glade
for you may see the fine elusive shade
of Silvia where moths of moonlight play
on willows drifting in a woodland pool.
No dryad, just a simple forestwife
in patchwork gown who lived a hermit's life
in harmony with Nature. Pure and cool
she gathers healing herbs with fingered grace
to tend the creatures of the earth and skies,
white magic flowing from her hands, her wise
young eyes compassionate. Within this place
her spirit lingers. Veiled in silver light
she sings her timeless songs through endless night.

Rosemarie Morton

SOUL-SEARCHING

Do you feel that life should be just for believing,
Accepting what others have said and put down?
Do you feel there is hope in sleeping and dreaming
Not questioning the feelings of doubt that have grown?

Are you sure the other man's totally right
Because at the time it seemed a good plan?
Is your questioning forgotten and put out of sight,
Hoping he totally did if for man?

Aren't promises just only visions and sounds?
Isn't believing another name for hypocrisy
If it's not followed by seeds planted in grounds?
Isn't being and doing the only democracy?

Do you just take for granted your child and your wife?
Aren't seeds the deeds of a new way of life?

Joan E Blissett

JEEPNEY

(Transport in the Philippines is heavily dependent upon the ubiquitous jeepneys - originally reconstructed jeeps left by the US army after World War 2. The new, aluminium jeepneys are brightly painted, and decorated with a multitude of horses, mirrors and religious aphorisms.)

The souped-up army-surplus Willys jeep's
A wurlitzer, all filigree and glitz.
It carries ten, plus - in the boondocks - sheep,
Coconuts and fighting cocks. The driver sits,
His Dodgers' cap reversed, a languid wrist
Draped casually, for effect, over the spare,
Part circus master, part somnambulist.
Almond-eyed girls in dazzling T-shirts stare
Straight ahead, avoid the lecherous eyes
Of slim-moustached Manila slickers.
Heavy with sampaguita and accessories,
The people carrier flaunts its holy stickers.
A priest rides shotgun as the driver, Ikey,
Steers, with one hand, his country's glittering psyche.

Norman Bissett

SMILE AGAIN SWEET MAIDEN

I saw you standing there holding flowers to your face,
It was a scene of beauty and peaceful grace,
You looked and smiled then my heart took wings,
As if the whole garden is a sonnet that sings.
If one could only such beauty embrace,
To feel the perfume of the flower, to love bring,
Comparing you with those Grecian muses entering,
Would be of one who would compose the tune apace.

Smile again sweet maiden that I might feel
A heart pounding within me spelling out the words,
A poet might write when upon this scene would steal
Comparing it to the sonnet of the flowers that is heard,
Echoing, echoing like the sound of a trumpet's peal,
Then love is like a soul with golden wings inspired.

John Clarke

ANTICIPATING SPRING

Will spring ever come visiting again
With daffodils nodding in the meadow?
Will I feel her clean softly scented rain
Washing away winter's dreary shadow?

The sun is selfish with her warmth this year
Reluctant to fan the flames of young life.
Griping in ice, the northern hemisphere
While angry winds cut sharply like a knife.

Will she arrive suddenly one bright day
Chasing cruel winter from hearts and mind?
Petals unfurling, tempting bees to play
Among blooms of the honey making kind.

Yes, she'll be here, one morning when I rise;
Therein, what grand anticipation lies.

Valerie McKinley

SILENT SOUND

I know there's such a thing as silent sound
I feel the sound the leaf makes when in flight
I see the sound of water and of light
I understand the sound made in the ground.
I hear the crocus, and I feel I've found
the colour of the robin sounds delight
and blackbirds' feet are sounding through my sight,
so what is in my senses all around?

It is not really in my sight at all
I do not hear a thing the normal way
the feeling of the leaf is just its fall.
How sound is all around I cannot say
but sound is inside me and holds me thrall
my silent sound is life, which calls me stay.

Hazel Harrison

GALLERY OF MODERN ART

A livid head of Lucian Freud stands out
Despite the subject's sausage-skin complexion.
A bust of Einstein and a Philipson,
The big Scotch landscape in the lower section,
Beside the cafeteria, the Christ
That ends the corridor, two Eardleys. The rest
Is balderdash and self-indulgent guff,
Offensive to the eye. The soul, depressed,
Hungers for beauty, truth to life, some sense
Of celebration and delight, but none
Is here. The melting phalluses and clocks
Are footling fooleries, all badly done.
The finest art the culture vulture sees
Outside the door, the avenue of trees.

Faith Bissett

REVELATION

Sunshine unwraps the mist from the hillside
Jagged rocks, lofty rocks, all clearly show
Buzzards and kites fly there, hunt and reside
Tumbling streams, bounding streams all swiftly flow.

Nothing now masked, mute with wonder and praise
Awesome scene, rustic scene, healing the mind
Nature on show, much opposing man's ways
Natural life, peaceful life, contentment find.

Seeking the sun is the human mind's goal
Lighting all, waking all, though clouds can mask
Giving some hope to encourage the soul
Seeking good, doing good, the human task.

Sunshine unwraps mist, from the swirling mind
Study perfection and peace you will find.

Wendy Dedicott

SECOND CHANCE

My heart cried, dreaming dreams of yore
What could have been, what would have been
Walking hand in hand, on a distant shore
Feelings honed to sharpness, slither keen

Thoughts and minds, entwined, as on a vine
Each mirroring each, in both our souls
I thought then, truly you were mine
But fate decreed, someone would pay me foul

The rift was deep and long between
The years of love, were very lean
Hope springs eternal, spring has sprung
The second chance has now begun

Maybe we'll stroll along that shore
Hand in hand for evermore.

Dora Watkins

LEARNING BY MISTAKE

When the bully boys cause too much abuse
And the powerful don't know what to do,
Those, in the know, fear it is too obtuse
In upsetting any more than the few.
When the very young are much too frantic
And the worldly wise are asked to dictate;
Where they cannot be over-pedantic,
They patiently wait for it to abate.
We all need good time to know a mistake
And by each experience do we learn.
The strife in life will give a cause to quake
And then for a private peace may we yearn.
Thus, with wise ones and sufferings will wars cease
And each one contribute to a world peace.

Susan Audrey

EARLY MORN

Shall I compare thee to the early morn?
Thou art more warmer and a lot more bright.
Harsh frosts do freeze the tiny rose thorn.
And the morning's sunrise is just like night.
Sometimes the morning comes far too soon.
And its coloured complexion truly dies.
The golden sunshine must give way to the moon.
But nature's course dims the rays that bathe thine eyes.
As time goes on the morning begins to fade,
And the glorious rays that shine on thy face.
Nature's ways must dim the morn that thou hast made,
But heaven's brightness sends us angelic grace.
So long as thee remains in thy memory,
Your life-giving image will remain with me.

Stephen Tuffnell

BEST FRIEND

A girl's best friend will tell her if she's fat,
Will help her choose a colour that's just right,
Will offer comfort when her boy's a 'rat',
Listening to tales of woe throughout the night.

A boy's best friend will lend a 'mate' his ear,
Will give advice to help him on a date,
He'll never steal a girlfriend from afar,
Or let him down or even make him late.

A man's best friend will offer strength and pride,
A woman's will become a second mother,
A man's best friend won't take him 'for a ride',
But my best friend is truly like no other.

As husbands go I'm blessed with whom I've got,
For my best friend's the best of all the lot.

K Jude

REJOICE

At a time of given choice,
Winter's artists paint the scene,
One and all, then rejoice,
As frost and snow, their impressions leave.

Merriment and joy, soon to come,
Remembering, re-visits, again,
Peace and sharing, for everyone,
Given of life, to forever remain.

Gifts exchanged, of thought-deserved,
Good will, the season of Christmas time,
Of memory, of the saviour's birth,
Candle-lights flicker, church bells chime.

At one year's death, that of another's birth,
A future's questions answered that
    Of the right to remain, unreserved.

Bakewell Burt

WE CAN SURVIVE

Can unrequited love ever survive?
I've decided you and I become we.
Already you've made up your mind to flee,
Leaving me alone in this wretched dive.
Thought you were the best looking person alive,
And you transformed my very days with glee.
Thought our relationship was meant to be,
I was sure our love would blossom and thrive.

But while you have left yet there is hope,
Do whatever it takes, hold onto you.
Because I will not sit around and mope,
Know I should change my ways, give me a clue.
It's time for talking, there's plenty of scope,
Want to remain with you, what must I do?

S Mullinger

LIFE'S POWER SUPPLY

If without power, where would we be,
Life in a turmoil, that's easy to see,
But what can we do when life's power goes flat,
Just connect up to Jesus it's as easy as that.

For we know for certain Christ's power won't fail,
So seek it today as you set on your trail,
Plus consider the pleasure of having it near,
And of power failures, you have nothing to fear.

The supply's always constant, not up and down,
Wherever you are, be it village or town,
So just stop and think do not delay,
Connect up to Jesus this very day.

And oh! What a bonus, no charges to pay,
How can I do it, I hear you say,
Just pray for connection, he will do the rest,
Put faith in His guidance, and give of your best.

Will A Tilyard

A CHANCELLOR'S TORMENT

Why didn't you die in forty five
  you lot that served in the war,
we've given you wheel chairs to help you survive
  yet still you keep asking for more.

Just what do you want, you pathetic old things
  can't you see that your use has long gone,
it isn't as if you've got your wings
  you're all old and some sixty years on.

So hurry and die, you pathetic has-been
  you've had your parades and the glor,
we've given you pensions and helped your hygiene,
  good clutches and medals galore.

So please just keep quiet you stupid old goats
but be there on call, when we ask you to vote.

Leslie Holgate

THANKFULNESS

Holy Lord, whose love diurnal
Is mine each returning dawn -
King of glory, God eternal
Be with me when the day is born.

I bow to thee with contrite heart -
All praise and honour to Thy name;
Almighty one, 'How great thou art',
Son of God, for sinners slain.

From thee alone comes help in stress,
Strength to bear our grief and sorrow,
All our sins thou dost redress
With promise of our great tomorrow
Our everlasting friend and guide,
Be Thou always by our side.

Marcella Pellow

THE STORM

The birds cease to sing
The sky goes dark
The dark clouds come down low
The wind picks up speed
And the rivers speed their flow
The clouds grow black and look very heavy
The lightning strikes quietly in the sky
Waiting for the thunder to roll
The thunder rolls the lightning strikes
And the rain comes pouring down
People run for shelter anywhere they can
People close their curtains and turn on all their lights
The windows rattle, gates bang to and fro
The birds shelter in the trees and cease to fly
The rabbits and the stoats seek shelter too
The grubs and worms go down in the ground
The storm is over, the world comes back to life
The birds shake their feathers and flap their wings
Then all of a sudden they start to sing
Their beautiful songs fill the air
The clouds lift and turn to white
The sun peeps through on the blue sky line
People open their windows and come out doors
The gates stop banging to and fro
Oh! What a lovely sight to see
The flowers open up to the sun and the children run around in fun
What a lot we have to thank the Lord for.

C Carr

PAPER ROSES

The wind blows
She clasps her woven shawl
Around her shoulders
As she carries a basket of paper roses

Hair in a long pig tail
Smile lights up a freckled face
She walks the roads, petite, frail
Wet roads, dry roads, rugged roads

Selling roses, paper roses
Alone in the world
Sheltering from life's storms
Hiding behind a shawl of obscurity

Walking the roads alone
Happy, secure in her simple cottage home.

Frances Gibson

HEAVEN DIVIDED

A midwife pens her ink upon the score,
the fountain breathes up sprinklets to the moon,
butterflies among the herbs quaver more, more
the sparrow gives vibrato soon, too soon.

Diving naked into canal sighs
the youth clean, spare and with unbroken line
one stolen fancy, death, birthright's eyes
by gondola Cornetto almost mine.

Antique leather, ancient statues wreathed
the ink too dry to stain my fingertips
a book of leaves so many pages breathed
the wine that bleeds with opiates on my lips.

The stars that twinkle over crib and hay
send down their tears and whisper peace, today.

Jennifer Hawthorne

A LIFE ONCE SHARED

Living in a world where pain won't leave me
I feel so all alone
Broken by a promise that deceived me
This life feels now so cold
Swallowed in the memories of the songs she sang
When our hearts felt then so young
I feel as if again I'll always wonder
What our future could have brung.

If only I could find that life she gave me
Again would beat this heart
Flowing on the fuel of life's emotions
As strong as from its start
Growing through a fire that lights the eyes
Of the ones who read the lines
Following the rules of love's emotions
For all who see the signs.

Never will we share again a sunset
Like the ones we shared before
All the colours falling into darkness
Like the ones that fell before.
Again I say goodbye and turn
Though I always look once more
Until again I bring more flowers
For your grave just as before.

Jason Glennon

ALL IS FORGOTTEN

Upon the heath the wind doth blow
against the green-eyed grass.
The nightly stars, a glaze, a glow
from days begone and past

Upon the hills the rain doth fall
against the white-eyed mist.
The nightly bird, a crying call
from the elements lingering twist

Upon the land the sun doth shine
against the yellow-eyed morn.
The warmth creates a sacred shrine
from new days being born

But all these tranquil things must bend
as man creates the world to end.

Lindsey Knowles

CONTENTMENT

Limited wealth, best not to gloom
Look for the inexpensive pleasures
Life can still be in full bloom
Good health is worth more than material treasures

Make the most of the situation
Adapt for life as it would unfold
Work for a better expectation
A close family bond is lasting gold

Learning as one grows older
Happiness of the whole is the plan
Decision making becomes more bolder
Contentment, grasp it when you can

Wealth varies the world over
What price is a true lover?

Brian Bates

THE GIRL ALONE

The days are broken, as the walls are high;
Pushing her inwards to a silent world.
No help is forthcoming; she hides her cries,
Lying in the darkness, in bed she's curled.

Thoughts will keep racing, out of her control,
As she commands herself to be more still.
Her heart is rapid and burns like hot coals,
With a tear in her eye, she feels so ill.

It seems like there is nobody to care,
Her friendships were lost - her moans were a bore.
Each time she goes out, the people will stare,
Searching for love, and there is not much more.

The days turn to months; the months turn to years,
Building a prison to enclose her fears.

Phillip Stringer

BEAUTIFUL CREATION

Oh beautiful creation, God placed you in man's hand
In his divine wisdom, he made us part of his great plan
Man chose independence, he clearly made his stand
He thought he had the answers, so now he'd take command

Oh beautiful creation, not made by human hands
We're all in this together, why won't we understand
Our planet Earth is groaning, with all of our demands
Reckless man keeps on moaning, issuing greater commands

Oh beautiful creation, man's time for realisation
Everyone, let's make a stand for future generations
Caretakers of this planet, we'll stand in veneration
With praise and thanks, songs and dance for our liberation

Oh beautiful creation, God sees our situation
What we sow is what we reap, proved true by every nation

J Smyth

SEASONS OF LIFE

In the spring of life it begins, we are born
Growing and learning, beginning to understand
Feelings of happiness, tears of sadness when death we morn
Love waiting for that special someone we take by the hand

In the summer of life, our children they play
It is up to us now to do our very best
Teaching and guiding, being there to show the way
Pride and love overwhelms us, we feel so blessed

In the autumn of life, time now to reflect
Where did we come from, where do we go
Our past actions just who did they effect
These answers to our questions we may never know

In the winter of life when all is done
We await our last journey home one by one by one.

Sallyanne Hayes

JUST ANOTHER DAY

Dark skies, heavy rain, pouring, blowing down
A single woman, out walking her dog
Rain's now so heavy, look out with a frown
See a few birds and a pond seeking frog

Plenty of puddles for kids to splash in
Soon they will be out in wellies and macks
But till the rain stops they're being kept in
Then they will pour out in bright shiny hats

At last the sky's clearing, sun's breaking out
A ray of warmth makes its way through the cloud
A rainbow appears, all the kids shout
The silence now gone, the kids way too loud

Puddles all shrink as the sun does its job
Plenty of folk now, no pond seeking frog.

John Cobban

A FATED STAR

A ship leaves Southampton water today,
The day is bright, the crowds, they gather in.
The new paintwork shows the White Star inlay,
America bound, a new life to win.

From top to bottom a wondrous sight,
Such a great ship the world has never seen.
The third class has food and parties each night,
She is fit indeed for the king and queen.

Nearly at the end of their voyage one night
What the lookout sees, it makes him go cold.
An iceberg, it drifts straight into his sight,
Many people it stops from getting old.

The Titanic left people in disgrace
When she sank that April without trace.

Anne Hayes (13)

A New Day

On his tiny shoulders is the world's weight.
Stone cold eyes view the best years of his life.
An emotional knot. A mental state.
Some last till death and know not of such strife.

Each night in his bed he waits for the door.
Like a military drum, his heart pounds.
He can tell by the force that shakes his floor.
If the energy's there to give ten rounds.

From slam to pain gets quicker by the day.
He closes his eyes and hopes for the best.
He'd cover his face but that's not the way.
He never gets hit higher than his chest.

'Sorry' would come with the rise of the sun.
'Forget what's happened, our new life's begun.'

Michael Robertson

NEAR DEATH

Death draws closer, the darkness guides its hand.
To steal your final breath, soul left to fate.
With body still strong, why desert this land?
No will to hide, vulnerable you wait.

So desperate for you to feel my love.
Your ears are closed to my words of hope.
Prayers turned to the heavens above,
In hope to please give you strength to cope.

Such cold air, a chill passes through the room.
Do not leave, do not take the hand of death.
Your eyes almost lifeless, mirrors of gloom.
Light, warmth, comfort you take another breath.

You've survived this brush with death, you live.
The Lord agrees, you have so much to give.

Marie O'Driscoll

SHIPYARD BLUES

A man outside the ailing shipyard gates
hesitates . . . and stares at the crane above,
unaware of the gossip of work mates:
and recalls the crane, as his first great love.
Once thriving shipyard, now a massive loss,
reduntified down, by the dockland's whore,
whose reign, for a time, didn't give a toss;
but in her short reign, rendered grown men sore.
Only looking forward to Friday night -
the pub - where he can vent his frustration
by bevvying, until he is well tight:
proudly enhancing his reputation.
But redundancy still preys on his mind;
and contentment, is rather hard to find.

Morgan Stuart

FACADE

There is a building that, as I sometimes
pass, leaves a particular impression
upon my mind. Deemed by those who study
such arts to be a fine example of
its kind, a real beauty to behold. This
building, however, is worn and old, in
need of some repair. Perhaps it is through
neglect that it crumbles now and falls. Too
beautiful to redesign; destruction
not allowed. Conservation resembled
against the grain of Nature's toll. Now it
stands an empty shell, only scaffold housed.

An outward appearance maintained complete:
at all costs, the facade must be preserved.

Rabbit Wallis

MYSTERY MAN

'The beauty of having a mystery man
Is nobody knows.'
You can be with him at ease,
While the world spins by
With a breeze.
Enjoying each other's company,
Talking and laughing.
Dining and wining and
Making plans. Nothing heavy.
'No demands.'
Caring for each other, so deep,
Caressing, until we fall asleep,
Simple things in measure,
Of hard work or pleasure,
It's the little things that count.
Me, I love my mystery man
Love, I have an endless amount
But then again, I believe in space.
'It's all part of the human race.'
Something to talk about and,
'How's your day?'
That's an important thing I
Must say.

Caroline Janney

SNOW

It comes as if driven by wild horses
Galloping through the night,
Bringing such dynamic forces
Covering everything in sight.
Yesterday the grass was greener
Now it's deathly white,
Making ridges on the branches
Drifts upon the ground,
People skidding, taking chances
Just to get around.
Yet it lies so peaceful now,
So soft, so pure, so white,
Creating picture postcard images
Through the day and night.

E M Gough

THE WOES OF WAR

We forget too soon the woes of war
As heroes they faced their enemies, brave and tall
In the muddy trenches, soiled hands, the bloodshed gore
The suffering and the misery endured throughout it all

Sentenced as a condemned man
Never knowing when
Life would cease to function in the cold brutal plan
Along with their comrade, country fellow men

Lined up young soldiers all in lines
They answered to their ill-fated destiny
Monuments of stone, a symbolic religious shrine
Rustic reminders of yesteryear's testimonial.

There they lay beneath wooden crosses
Countless victims, war's unnecessary losses.

R E Humphrey

EDEN

Woken from a slumber that was so deep
I look upon your face and smile;
as you take my hand, you're now complete,
and you want to walk awhile.

This garden fills me with delight,
with smells so strange and fresh,
that animals bound and birds take flight
as we walk in naked flesh.

As you sleep, I see a tree so
beautiful, tall and strong,
that I don't see the serpent sliding low,
and whispering, 'You know it can't be wrong.'

First bite you took, my sight came clear,
as I saw innocence lost and knew mortal fear.

Kathy Hill

THE LOOK

Be frank with me, and look into my eyes,
Shift not your sight in furtive flight from mine,
But eye to eye let understanding rise,
To set your gaze in surely holding mine.

Can you, I wonder, live in open mood,
And pulse for pulse join with my every beat;
Or will you wander in a darkened wood,
Where searching glances spread your wild retreat?

Will you open the window of your soul?
To let me read overtly in the book
That is your heart - the stored secluded whole -
Whether you'll ever trade an honest look?

For could your stare be with integrity,
It could ensnare and truly capture me.

C S Mantle

WOT! NO BEDS

A stay in hospital is not a happy prospect
But ill health determines you must go
Then looking on the bright side one thinks positive
The rest, the comforts, served food and warm glow

Comes the day when I am stretchered out
By personnel who know what it's all about
'Been waiting long?' asked one man nodding his head
'Indeed I have, eight months for a hospital bed.'

'Never mind,' this cheery chap assured me
'You'll soon be where it's cosy and warm, you'll see!'
At hospital they wheeled me in on a trolley
And in the corridor put the brake on hard

'That was seven weeks ago and my words I do not mince.
But believe me when I tell you I've been on that
                    trolley ever since!'

Charles Meacher

IF I SHOULD

If I should lose my love for life, and be
No longer happy, both in thought or ways;
Or if my senses leave so that I see
My independence fading in a haze:
If I should lose my faculties and find
I need the help of others to exist,
Or if confusion stupefies my mind
And leaves my senses shrouded in its mist:
If I should feel as living takes its toll
And age begins to thin my bones and breath
The ghoul of pain's expanding in my soul
Before it's been prepared for facing death:

Take care of me, and when with sleep I'm blessed,
Help me find peace, wherever I may rest.

Nicholas Winn

SECRET GARDEN
(A sonnet in the Italian style)

Compute this inter-planetary scene:
A space administration, blind with pride,
Ensures its astronauts enjoy the ride.
The search is on to find the extra gene,
They have to take this bigger step foreseen.
The silver angel points to Martian bride
As plasma-thrusters flash the farther side.
Thus, human-kind now vents its simple spleen.

Alien disenchantment with this Earth
Spreads further on, man's inter-stellar need,
On parchment of new heaven to find worth,
In shining-shuttle dandelion seed.
To gods, this great red-planet will give birth,
In Eden number two . . . should they succeed.

Roger Mosedale

THIS MAN

Could this be love I am not quite sure.
Though I do like him very much.
I need a love that's strong and true.
From a man with a sensitive touch.

Following an accident I've been wheel chair bound
Trapped for months longing for my freedom to walk again.
At last I'm recovered now, safe and sound
Now able to walk through fields refreshed by summer rain.

Silent love has a voice only I can hear.
Lips so sweet, no roughness there.
His kiss so tender on my cheek I wept fresh tears.
This man has made my heart aware.

This man of steel with rugged looks
Sends a shiver down my spine.
So sensitive, kind, a great reader of books
I'm so glad to say he's mine.

I couldn't resist the love you see, from this honest and gentle man
This man I met was meant to be not from any calculated plan.

Pamela Margaret Wild

HOW FAIR IS OUR LOVE?

Is there a love as fair, my dear?
Or any rose as sweet?
Could my heart beat as fierce as fear?
When first our two souls meet?

Do others see the posies?
That bloom beneath our feet?
Could others sense this closeness?
When first our eyes did meet?

Can you capture dewdrops?
Could their nectar taste as sweet?
Can you feel time slip to a stop?
When first our fingers meet?

Our two hearts choose to beat as one,
Because our mind, soul, spirit meet.

Christina Mallon (18)

SHOOTING STARS

From starry fields two meteors conspired
To leave the splendour of the Milky Way,
Freed from the galaxy's rotating spray,
Not stars but streaks of light from heaven fired.

The magic of their brilliance has inspired
Poets to write romantic roundelays,
Choosing each golden word and jewelled phrase
To honour maidens whom they most admired.

Like shooting stars our love blazed for a while,
And incandescent dust blinded our eyes
With radiance both bright and volatile
That dazzles then consumes itself and dies.
But new love brings new light, makes life worthwhile,
And from the ash a phoenix can arise.

Celia G Thomas

MOZART'S OWN REQUIEM

You wrote your requiem; from what vast deep
Did you hear harmony beyond all thought?
The guiding stars in silence vigil keep,
The land is stilled in silence sundown brought.
We cannot hear the song beyond the sun,
Catch a faint echo, at the break of day,
Or in the dying light when day is done
From somewhere past those farthest stars away.
You heard the music from beyond the world:
Not wind, nor mountain-stream, nor surging sea
At sunrise, the great golden clouds unfurled,
So like high heaven's immortal song can be.
The pale light fades, day's murmur dies: through all
The silent shadows waiting angels call.

Diana Momber

SHALL I?

Shall I liken you to the sweet primrose
to be compared surely a fragrant gift
another breath of springtime to hold in prose
an everlasting rainbowed colour drift

Shall I adore the image disarmingly portrayed
pale moon accentuating with delicate air
sun-rays streaming as a shadowed array
to acclaim the vision of silken hair

Shall you reciprocate by inward grace
glance at me perhaps in a favourable way
though light fails to enhance my weary face
distorting rotund shapes not held at bay

Shall we some day be one my dearest love
or drift apart awhile as the lonely dove . . .

Margarette L Damsell

SAM'S DISTEMPER

'Twas a wretched scene for which the shepherd keened
His faithful hound now so direly quiet beside him,
For with his extinct crook, lay his shattered flock:
In ruthless slaughter in the fields surrounding.
For upon this year had descended a savage scourge
Like some ancient plague of Moses.
Come to strip the land, and tax the dreams of man:
Like some dreadful swarm of locust.
So upon vales laid bare, did summer stare
Spring's clement flower on the pyres there blazing,
The sacrificial pall of the distemper's toll:
In aspect like the dark spectre stalking.
So before the altars, shall we our matins raise;
And there petition heaven and the Lord for grace.

M Dixon

Sonnet On A Dead Mouse In A Trap

There lies he dead, and in his unseeing eyes
Is mirrored still the horror of his end.
He ventured forth, too hungry to be wise,
And saw too late the fatal spring descend.

Who knows what agonies he suffered there,
His broken body writhing neath the steel,
While at his whiskers end the cheesy snare
With teasing odour mocked at his ordeal.

His life was innocent compared with man's,
He was but what God fashioned him to be -
A helpless victim of relentless plans,
Abhorred in life, and dead a theme for glee.

Yet had he been but born to dog's estate,
The whole world would have sorrowed at his fate.

R Probert

HEN NIGHTERS

We are in the right mood to go and be silly, out-,
- have thrown off work suits, sensibles, and out we dart.
The dismissive will always have their shout,
- we hen on, scented in 'Here's my heart'.

Inside the dancing dens, gloom is now barred.
After pours of rosé, we champagne to floor.
Outside, are the fight-stoppers, and they're real hard;
marinated in perspiration, we'll bop till four.

Gaggle-mellow, we're on a moon-crashed avenue,
slurring steps, though can still do fun, joy, song.
Where we've left our shoes, we haven't a clue;
Back in wife-coats, we get the kettle on.

Friday night's special . . . it's there for the fizz,
- till we creep back into what was and is.

L Liffen

SONNET TO A GARDEN

Now enters March; the gardener's year begins,
yet winter's frost still lingers with its chill,
made worse across the frozen heath the winds
send shivers round each trembling daffodil.

But soon, I know and see with inward eye,
the promise e'en a lazy spring can give.
As warm Earth stirs and wintry gusts must die,
each plant's rebirth - a promise it will live.

With watchfulness and tender loving care,
I give my troth, that I will do my part,
when roses bloom and honeysuckle fair,
their fragrant scents forever in my heart.
Though simple flower, or wond'rous plant so rare,
what else has such fulfilment to impart?

Sylvia Shepherd

SUMMER'S SONG

When frost is on the meadows long
And cold has taken power
All winter long the bloom has gone
I droop, I cringe and cower.
When the sun is strong and days are long
I bloom just like a flower
I sing along with summer's song
And thrive in summer's bower
When life's short season's gone, and I am further on
You will find me with the flowers
In summer's song where I belong
In warm and peaceful hours
The warmth of His love shall sustain me
My soul forever free.

Fred Battye

HOW GREAT MY LOSS

It's hard when it's in your face
Hearing those words, some stranger said
Your mother's gone, left this worldly place
I'm so sorry to tell you, your mother's dead
We did all we could dear, but she was old
She'd had a good innings at ninety-one
Her time had come, just spent and cold
You must accept my dear, your mother's gone
I heard his words, but just couldn't bear
His cold remarks about my closest friend
Cutting words so deep, for what did he care
I couldn't foresee, her dear life would end
I'd loved her so, and I knew my great cost
Of that someone so special, I'd just lost.

Ann Hathaway

HAVE YOU THE WILL?

We Poetry Now Anchor Books Women's Word
are challenging poets to try and get
their ti tum ti tum into verses heard
and ask would you like to write a sonnet?

Fourteen lines rhyme in a specific manner
one rhymes with three and two rhymes with four
three four-lined verses is the sonnet's tanner.
Can you make your imagination soar?

Set out to present a proposition
from your experience in life that's fine
you will need a realistic conclusion
with a two-lined finale, this is mine.

I worked very hard to write my first sonnet
have you the will to pick up the gauntlet?

B A Jermyn

A 21ST CENTURY SONNET

Do you have some love for me or none,
can you find a way to let it show?
Was it all a great big con,
why to tell me of your love, are you so slow?

Just an occasional glimpse of it would suffice,
not all that often would it need to be returned.
Try saying 'I love you' just once or twice.
Why are my fingers so badly burned?

Indeed, I loved you,
and thought that love would never die.
There was nothing for you I wouldn't do.
Now it's in the past, gone by.

Believe me, I didn't want it to end this way.
Let's not hurt each other anymore, let's call it a day.

A'O'E'

WHAT IS A GARDEN!

What is a garden if not to be seen,
with wonderful flowers and grass so green.
Hard work and attention, plenty of care,
resulting in flowers, everywhere.
What is a garden if not to grow,
beautiful flowers to display and to show.
Pleasure and joy to all that should venture,
colourful garden, splendid adventure.
What is a garden if not to admire,
flame-like ornateness of roses in bloom,
filling the air with sweet smelling perfume.
Flowers bring solace to comfort and cheer,
for now and forever, year after year.
Plants of adornment in gardens so near.

Audrey Taylor

SONNET ON PRAYER

Who dares to say that prayers are never heard,
   That there's no deity - no God above?
Who says that all creation just occurred,
   With no great power behind it which can love?
'There's no Creator God,' these people say,
   'And 'answered prayers' are mere coincidence.'
A wise man wrote that when he ceased to pray
   Coincidences ceased to happen - hence
He must believe there is a God who cares
   For man, whom he created on this Earth.
How can we know that our Creator shares
   Humanity's concerns - to death from birth?
Because he chose to come, through Mary's womb,
Die on a cross, then rise from death's dark tomb.

Mabel Helen Underwood

HESITATION

Should I speak now of this consuming fire?
I hesitate and can't make up my mind.
Could I lose everything that I desire?
Because the words I need I cannot find.

If I could let my feelings rule my head,
and tell her how I've loved her from the start;
But wordlessly I moon about instead,
when I should bravely speak straight from the heart.

I think she really knows just how I feel,
and maybe the initiative she'll take;
Perhaps at her feet I should simply kneel,
and she will lift me up for my own sake?

I gaze into her eyes and there I see
encouragement and love awaiting me.

James Kimber

CRY IN THE DARK

The door bangs, fracturing uneasy peace.
The voices muffled, then with urgent strains.
One smack, one cry, then begging for release.
A chair falls, then a shout and silence reigns.

My heart pounds and my stomach clenches tight
As I wait the footstep on the stair.
The dreaded creak will come and I will fight
To stem the scream that wants to rend the air.

Yet, as I lie there, silence flows around
And fills my head with unaccustomed calm.
And now a noise, an unexpected sound
That soothes my soul with restorative balm.

A cry of joy and dare I now believe
Tomorrow's dawn and promise of reprieve?

Michele Cameron

MARTIN'S SONNET

Late, when each worried breast
by tossing and turning is eased of pain,
when orphans also in dream are blest,
of Laurie, uneasy, I complain.
The bright sun discards the dull of night,
its rays, the warmth, and morning return;
each of Heaven's creatures welcome the light,
whilst I, alone, sit and endlessly mourn.

At midday, I beg my mourn to cease,
the sun grows stronger, and my complaints increase,
and again at night my soul grieves -
the darkness returns, to mourning I renew,
never am I set free; struggling I sue,
night never releases, and Laurie never relieves.

Martin Mooney

FOR 'SONS' OF GOD . . .

A siren, trumpet, yellow lamps . . . night falls,
The broken down mind, in need of His balm:
The loneliest heart, hearing voices that call -
Sheltered in here, and inside . . . an alarm . . .

There's light and hope in Christ's loving peace -
There's moments of stillness, unwasted and spent
Unravelling knots, in the search for release,
With the focus on One, who knows all we vent . . .

The battle is thick, the foe knows no rules,
But the Lord has the vict'ry . . . inside;
The hearts and minds of those - who are fools
Ignore Him with their earthly pride . . .

I find my rest in his work to be done -
This frail, feeble vessel . . . known as, His son.

Richard D Reddell

CROSSROADS

If indecision clouds your mind
When certain choices must be made,
Be still - a true way you will find.

Take time to let yourself unwind,
Be calm - let calmness be your aid
If indecision clouds your mind.

Resist the urge to follow blind,
Allow your choice to be delayed,
Be still - a true way you will find.

Remain unswayed by ties that bind,
Be honest - never be afraid
If indecision clouds your mind.

One day you'll leave the past behind,
Just wait until your doubts all fade,
Be still - a true way you will find.

Be faithful to yourself - be kind
Until your sun dispels the shade,
If indecision clouds your mind
Be still - a true way you will find.

Katrina Shepherd

VILLANELLE

My love has gone away from me
Whatever can I do?
I'll find her wherever she may be.

Our family miss her gaiety,
And yet she's left no clue:
My love has gone away from me,

I've yet to see,
What I can do,
I'll find her wherever she may be.

Her laugh lingers with me;
And her sparkling eyes so blue,
My love has gone away from me.

Let us see what we can do,
To resolve this saga through;
I'll find her wherever she may be.

The hope I have will give to thee,
The love I have for you,
My love has gone away from me,
I'll find her wherever she may be.

J Townsley

WINTER AND SPRING

The winter drew a curtain grey
To shroud the frozen land, until
Spring briefly pulled the folds away.

Clouds raced in to hide the ray
Of sunshine, and, with laughter shrill,
The winter drew a curtain grey.

Upon the barren ground there lay
A pall of frozen grass, but still
Spring briefly pulled the folds away.

The pale earth begged that she would stay,
But, as he gripped with harsher chill,
The winter drew a curtain grey;

With ice and snowflakes he would play.
But, eager yet to have her will,
Spring briefly pulled the folds away.

In welcome to the quickening day,
A robin sang with quivering bill;
The winter drew a curtain grey,
But spring, she pulled the folds away.

Margaret Ballard

City Canal

Still birds swim over the rainbow
That will fade with passing time
Bruised depths moving slow

The banks are high, the water low
Oiling slick turned bathtub rime
Still birds swim over the rainbow

Narrowboats passing to and fro
Cutting through the surface slime
Bruised depths moving slow

Sunday strolling on the tow
Trying to see beyond the grime
Still birds swim over the rainbow

Abandoned car, discarded barrow
Surreptitious acts of crime
Bruised depths moving slow

Green canal now wreathed in sorrow
Unwanted, wasted past its prime
Still birds swim over the rainbow
Bruised depths moving slow.

Jan Edwards

NONSENSE RHYME

My shadows the oldest companion I know
It never lets me down
And stays with me wherever I go

It never says I told you so
And never wears a frown
It's mine and mine alone you know

It has to go wherever I go
And can move just like a clown
It can both shrink and grow

As we both move to and fro
Both there and back from town
It never tells me where to go

Yes! My shadow's the oldest companion I know
Never letting me down
And never ever seems to care
If my skin is white or brown.

Audrey E Ritzkowski

STIRRED AND LIFTED

Hearts are lifted in the spring
The garden blooms anew
As nature stirs for her annual fling.

Spirits soar are given wings
One thinks of summer sun
Hearts are lifted in the spring.

Trumpets blow and bells they ring
Buds burst forth in song
As nature stirs for her annual fling.

Lambs arrive the birds they sing
Nesting time is here
Hearts are lifted in the spring.

All around bare earth will bring
Colour bright and gay
As nature stirs for her annual fling.

The winter days will soon be past
Summer's on the way at last
Hearts are lifted in the spring
As nature stirs for her annual fling.

F L Brain

TOGETHER WE'LL STAND

My love and I stay hand in hand.
Death attempted to make us part.
Together throughout time we'll stand.

Our lives are bound with a gold band
To form one whole, one mind, one heart.
My love and I stay hand in hand.

With joy, our ship of love was manned;
Soulmates our map of life we'd chart.
Together throughout time we'll stand.

Laughter filling sails, love's flame fanned,
Not pierced by arrow or sharp dart;
My love and I stay hand in hand.

One partner's gained the promised land.
Though division makes my eyes smart,
Together throughout time we'll stand.

No one can break what God has planned.
In Heaven our new lives will start.
My love and I stay hand in hand;
Together throughout time we'll stand.

Wendy A Nottingham

WE DWELL ON EARTH

We dwell on Earth and live our span
Working living caring
We are God's creation. Man.

With Adam and Eve it all began
Woman born for child bearing
We dwell on Earth and live our span

Trying to do the best we can
Doing deeds so daring
We are God's creation. Man.

We all want the bomb to ban
Give 'our' views an airing
We dwell on earth and live our span

Sit in the sun and get a tan
Sometime 'our' souls baring
We are God's creations. Man.

Have been since the world began
Eyes uplifted into the heavens staring
We dwell on Earth and live our span
We are God's creation. Man.

June Clare

DEAR JUDY - A VILLANELLE

Dear Judy is to London flown,
in Upper Richmond Road is she,
to live alone, yet not alone,

for flats and habitations shown
by many an urgent Agency.
Dear Judy is to London flown,

her flat for sale, its value grown;
a garden is where she would be,
to live alone, yet not alone.

We drove, with many a silent moan,
to catch her train at ten to three;
Dear Judy is to London flown.

Pub lunch of egg and chips, I own,
and then, a kiss. She turned to flee,
to live alone, yet not alone.

With letters, e-mails and the 'phone,
heart-filled with friends she'll ever be.
Dear Judy is to London flown
to live alone, yet not alone.

Anthony Duncan

HOPE IS FADING NOW

Hope is fading now and with it my dreams,
Thoughts of you and I becoming one.
I've lost the chance of endless love it seems.

Only in memory and what those memories mean
The treasured store of things we've said and done.
Hope is fading now and with it my dreams.

No more time with you to boost my self-esteem,
No more days together, no more fun.
I've lost the chance of endless love it seems.

I long for you, my mind and body screams.
The pain of losing you goes on and on.
Hope is fading now and with it my dreams,
I've lost the chance of endless love it seems.

Joyce Walker

THE LAST BUTTERFLY

No more her beauty will I see,
no more her wings to fly,
she promised not eternity,

how deep my love, my love for thee,
a love so strong, could only death deny,
no more her beauty will I see

fate came and stole my love from me,
our vows no more will echo the sky,
she promised not eternity

angels cry their timeless plea,
that life and love should never die,
no more her beauty will I see,

now my world is but a memory,
where beside me once did beauty lie,
she promised not eternity,

comes the dawn, the sun breaks free,
soft upon the breeze a whispered goodbye,
no more her beauty will I see,
she promised not eternity.

Jim Cuthbert

HERE TO STAY

I never want to go away
I always want to be with you
Because my love is here to stay.

I neither care what people say
Nor do I mind what people do
I never want to go away.

I mean to stay with you each day
My old behaviour is all through
Because my love is here to stay.

The past now gone is stowed away
For now I'm older, wiser, too
I never want to go away.

I'll help you always come what may
I want to bear your burdens too
Because my love is here to stay.

My life, complete with you each day
The sky above is always blue
I never want to go away
Because my love is here to stay.

Irene Foxcroft

A VILLANELLE

I walk this store with dresses along
To see the dresses on their hanging rack
T'was so exciting I burst into song

Here I am humming my song
When seeing a shopper wearing a smock
T'was so exciting we burst into song

There you are singing my song
There they are having a snack
T'was so exciting we started to jig along

They are walking as they shop along
T'was so exciting they started to mock
For we were singing a well written song

Sing on! Sing on! A merry song
We are in this store to view your flock
Then barter as we select along

Listen, listen then dance along
Read my lyrics then buy my stock
Dance to my music for they're singing my song
Clap our hands as we sing along.

Dalsie Mullings

A SOUL IN DESPAIR

The pain in my heart is as heavy as stone
Our parting proved too much to bear
How I wish I was back home!

The pain subsides but I still moan
I should have shown her that I care
The pain in my heart is as heavy as stone

The strength and support I need is on loan
From others I will draw and share
How I wish I was back home

My mind is still in turmoil thrown
I can't find peace anywhere
The pain in my heart is as heavy as stone

It drives me crazy this being alone
The loneliness causes such despair
How I wish I was back home

The words spoken cut me to the bone
I still smell the perfume she would wear
The pain in my heart is as heavy as stone
How I wish I was back home.

M B Powell

OUR LOVELY MUM

Many moons since you slipped away,
Still silently weep every day,
Often long to turn back tideway.

In our mannerisms you stray,
Living on in speech and display,
Many moons since you slipped away.

Yearn to share with you a heyday,
To receive solace on mayday,
Often long to turn back tideway.

When in doubt muse what you would say
Or do to keep trouble at bay,
Many moons since you slipped away.

All is calm then flares in flambé
When void you left comes into play,
Often long to turn back tideway.

Life is enacting own screenplay,
Coping with roles that fall our way,
Many moons since you slipped away,
Often long to turn back tideway.

Hilary Jill Robson

VILLAIN-HELL

Emotions now are galvanised,
As dawns the truth you love me not;
No more can I my pain disguise.

The demons I must exorcise
In hope to quell, dispel and blot . . .
Emotions now are galvanised.

As fear draws shade o'er tearful eyes,
It pains to know he loved me not;
No more can I my pain disguise.

Must learn to live and know it wise
To live with what he fast forgot;
Emotions now are galvanised.

This love-free zone of space implies
How bullet-sweet the lies you plot;
No more can I my pain disguise.

Your fierce assault of red-hot lies
Burn down the dreams not built to rot:
Emotions now are galvanised;
No more can I my pain disguise.

Linda Zulaica

THE MILLER

The stream runs down from dale and hill.
I step out of the grinding race.
Beside the oak an ancient mill.

A stony stream so clear in will.
No labour now just freedom's place.
The stream runs down from dale and hill.

No corn is ground the wheel is still.
Tranquillity reforms my face.
Beside the oak an ancient mill.

The miller's life beside the gill.
Released his ghost a dusty trace.
The stream runs down from dale and hill.

Though time has moved and trumpets shrill.
My heart beats slow with water's pace.
Beside the oak an ancient mill.

I rooted stay and drink my fill
Till I can feel the miller's grace.
The stream runs down from dale and hill.
Beside the oak an ancient mill.

Steve Emsley

I AM YOUR ROCK

I am your rock, that you can cling to, in a storm,
your nurse in sickness, and carer through infirmity,
a pair of arms that forever keep you safe and warm,

all the love and attention will now and always adorn,
God has smiled on us, to give you charm and beauty,
I have truly loved you from the day you were born,

there was never another, a danger of ever being torn,
it's my privilege to be there for you, in fact my duty,
to be with you all the days, from each and every morn,

your looks to me, are a true delight, whatever is worn,
in my eyes, you are my treasure, my darling, eternally,
run to me if you need to, I'll be here, to dusk from dawn,

whenever you are away, think of me, and never be forlorn,
whatever you do, you will do with appeal, and beautifully,
wherever you may be, to you I will be constantly drawn,

I will love you without end, so will you, keeping to form,
love me like I love you, with all the elegance I can see,
without you in my thoughts and soul, I would surely mourn,
caress my hand, and kiss my lips, my rose without a thorn.

Christopher Higgins

NAMELESS AND FAMELESS

I am that of what? I'm nameless:
Of this blooded earth search blindfold;
Called to mind am not! I'm fameless.

The life I've lead - this life is aimless,
An existence to which I hold;
I am that of what? I'm nameless.

This world surrounds - I find frameless
Covered with its tainted fools gold;
Called to mind am not! I'm fameless.

The crime committed - I'm blameless,
A child of five is often told;
I am that of what? I'm nameless.

The fire that flickers is flameless
With smocking embers - found them cold;
Called to mind am not! I'm fameless.

Faced with darkness I'll be shameless;
Youth rages but inside grows old,
I am that of what? I'm nameless:
Called to mind am not! I'm fameless.

Marcus Tyler

PUTTING ON THE STYLE

This is us, putting on the style,
Creating poems by their jingle,
And thinking, writing all the while.

Fair poets are know as versatile,
And words which they mix and mingle.
This is us putting on the style.

Rhyming words hatch a crafty guile,
Like a demon gives a tingle,
And thinking, writing all the while.

Now you may laugh or you may smile,
Sat in the nook by the ingle.
This is us putting on the style

With Beelzebub, the time to wile,
All of us, married or single,
And thinking, writing all the while,

But not so sweet as Tate and Lyle,
As you may see with this *swindle*.
This is us putting on the style
And thinking, writing all the while.

William Sheffield

THE BALLAD OF SUNSHINE VALLEY

The dawn awoke with a twinkle of an eye
In Sunshine Valley years gone by
It was sweet Belle who told us the tale
How her lover Bertram called in the vale

Belle lived quite near to the Sunshine Valley
That is how she became so very pally
He being a lad so fair and bright
Belle's family thought Bertram, just right

Bertram, Belle knew loved her so dearly
And they spent quite often, time in the valley
Planning their future together you see
When out of the blue, came a lass called Bee

Beatrice was her full ripe name
She came from the other side of Sunshine Valley
'Bertie what is your game?
So this is the lass that has come between
    thee and me'
Belle was heart-broken completely, you see

Now Belle goes it alone to the Sunshine Valley
No other beau did she find so pally
She wanders there at dawn to dally
It never occurred to her she was a
    proverbial wally!

Alma Montgomery Frank

THE ROAD TO SNOWDON

We started fair at Llangollen,
gateway to golden Snowdonia.
The bridge was built by famous men
and strode the fast racing river.

As we went, the hills glowed soft
yellow green and wandering white wool
dots blossomed all around and oft
they sipped the sky held in a pool.

We came at last to Horseshoe Pass
and met the early crystal snow.
Our dog was fast along the path,
leaping the grass and scenting low;

the rabbits ran amok. We braved
the blast, the frosty flakes and went
right to the top and pausing, gazed
at emerald earth till hearts were spent.

The perfect air made blood flow clear
and weary eyes rejuvenate.
The sound of silence, waiting near,
told us slowly of our fate.

Approaching Corwen by the oak,
we glimpsed the mighty peak.
A dreadful sense of awe awoke
in us as winter sun shone weak

and lit our way to lake
Bala. We crossed the Dee again
and lightness touched our step. Awake,
the call came pure and clear, begin

again, start fresh and new. Across
the tarn it touched the sky, mighty
Snowdon, cold and pink and gold, lost
in mystery's mist. Sunset nightly

had ever been and now it came
again. We saw the moon caress
its heights and softly speak its name.
With joyful tears, we went to rest.

Jack W Oliver